So What?

So What?

HAYDEN CHURCH

MAXIMUS BOOKS

NORTH · FLORIDA

2022

ISBN: 9798357801135 (paperback)

Published by Maximus Books in the USA.
First edition

To Alice Notley, Charles Olson, and Mao Zedong

I'd like to thank these publications who so kindly first published these poems, some in slightly different form:

Apocalypse Confidential: 'Killing Gomer Pyle,' 'Dress-Up,'
'There Is a Way Out,' 'My Son'
Azure Bell: 'Locating the Edge'
Bear Creek Gazette: 'The Great Possum'
Bruiser Magazine: 'Bunny Rabbit',
The Crank: 'Jackson County War 2,' 'One Thing'
Don't Submit!: 'So What,' 'Pig is Cow'
The Kudzu Review: 'Chickens'
Misery Tourism: 'Jackson County War,' 'Cattle,' 'There will be a time when you're all alone and there will be nothing you can do about it'
Safety Propaganda: 'Coup Détat,' 'In Translation'
Tragickal: 'Eau de Parfum'

CONTENTS

I

LIST OF ILLUSTRATIONS

front cover: *Peasant Girl with Dog* (Pierre-August Renoir), c. 1894, Cleveland Museum of Art; back cover: *Dog Urinating on Rock* (Dirk Valkenburg), c. 1695 – 1721, Art Institute of Chicago.

So What?

Jackson County War

AT 3 YEARS OLD, I held the hand of a Mrs. Lucinda Shapely, who was the wife of a Great Possum man in Marianna, residing in Jackson County, Florida. Our conversation was short because I was so young, but I remember potato salad with peas, which I never asked for again.

'We shall keep the things the same way that they are forever,' she told me, and I believed in her dream of blood that mattered for many years to me. Little could I have known that the Possums would become a great problem for me and my family.

Jackson County was in fact under the great province of The Great Possum Organization, due to several reasons that are socio-economical and tough to illustrate due to my lack of knowledge at my age (3). I hear, though, during what is now called the Reconstruction Era they was quite mad, the Great Possums. I could never quite understand being so angry about any subject, due to the stoic temperament instilled in me by my family.

The Possums were angry about how the Civil War had ended, and I gathered as much from my clippings from a newspaper with national syndication, in an attempt to make myself knowledgeable about all sides of the issue, that issue being, as I took it, a matter of policy, that policy being the practice of slavery in our state and several others that surrounded us. I am not certain what to make of it.

But Daddy, he was so glad the Civil War was over that he nailed that portrait of Abraham Lincoln against the wall, proud of how we was still here. We was slave owners, it is true, but to the credit of our family's resilience we gave it up easy because Daddy knew business well.

Daddy was an accountant at a bank, and grew up in old Alford. I was one year old at the time he taught me tabular analysis (for I was indeed a precocious child); he showed me the manner in which one calculates yield, what profits are, though I still do not understand it well. Mama was what was now called 'old money,' in Marianna. I have heard from several Negroes whom I trust in their spying and gossip that she was once fine card player on a showboat – 'the best in her day,' I am told by Gabby-Dear, who is one of my most dear friends around the house. I was saddened by Mama's insistence for awhile in her resolution to never play cards with us babies, for it was too difficult for her to let us win, but I do recall beating her several times on my own. Surely such events have been expunged from or outright forgotten about in the record books, another unfortunate thing one mustn't mention in the South.

IN THE MORNINGS, Gabby-Dear would wake me up and let me go see the chickens and horses and pigs – she would tell the pigs 'Git! Git! Git!' when they'd try to steal the feed from my hands. 'Times is hard with no help in these fields,' she tells me. I cannot say I disagreed with her assessment, but, as they say, things change. Gabby-Dear has never known her mother or her brothers or sisters or even her father.

In the evenings, James, who used to be our Overseer, gathered soft flowers from the pond and laid them next to the window at the morning gruel. James lived with us and is a wonderful writer of letters. He wrote a letter to my mother on one occasion which he left in my hiding place in the tree out back and I accordingly intercepted it. Contained inside it were sordid details and acts which I cannot even conceptualize, let alone act as scrivener in describing back to

4

you, in words. If that is what a 'man of letters' is, then I would like to be nothing of the sort. Ever since, I have made no mention of it to neither mother nor James nor father nor anyone except Remus, for he is my friend.

I do love Remus. He has been with our family since my brother William was born, before the War. His daughter is Baby Doll, with whom I like to go look at my Mama's garden and scare the possums away with a rake.

'Where's your mother, Baby Doll?' I would ask.

'She got kilt by some Possums,' she'd say. I was too young to know that she hadn't meant the rodent.

Gabby-Dear would take us babies out to the water and helped us look at our reflection in the water (she'd say, 'Cain't you see yo'self in there? It ain't you but issa a reflection of you') and later in the mornings, before lunchtime, she held me to her breast and held me tight, singing a soft song about the Old Days to me, a song of Old Dixie times, as Mama gathered my sisters Lucille and Mary-Ellen by their hair and tied them together in a cruel fashion of a game which I never understood.

ONE DAY I asked Remus if he remembers what things were like before the Civil War.

'Before? Why, ain't there always a before? Is not right now a before? Ain't it the same as now? Is not time indifferent to us as men are?'

I reckon I have no idea what that meant.

WHAT THEY NEVER tell you is when the next war will happen, so even at a young age such as I am (3), one must still prepare one's self mentally and physically for the act of war. I likely knew one would happen; the only variable I could not accurately control was time, when and where such an event would happen. As an expert at hiding around the estate, I knew well the layout and configuration of the entire plantation – or what was formerly one. I could calculate the exact angle necessary for the quick ascent to the top level of the barn, where we kept all the hay to feed the horses and various tools, like rakes and shovels, which we did not necessarily use too often on the farm as such – only in the worst part of summertime when we needed to dig everything up and plant anew. That was always the best place, but I knew others, like the workers' outhouse where no one much used it no more because most everyone used the field when they needed to go.

So, that was why I hid in the barn when the Possums tried to take our land. Remus – he was the one who told me to hide in the barn. I was small and fit under a sack, so I brushed the hay away, and the horses started kickin' up dust and made me choke, but I held it in and coughed like a horse so the men wouldn't know the difference between me and a horse. I remember the fire out in the fields from the barn and I started crying but Remus told me to hush it. I seen Baby Doll running down the road, screaming Hell. Men was chasing her. I don't know what happened to Baby Doll after that but I suspect I do.

Out on the porch after the fires I would listen to the frogs at night, I would count my marbles and put them in the pecan tree for Remus to find and return them with an impressively consistent resolve to never let me know he knew I placed them there, mother always crying in her rocking chair because we had William's funeral that week.

One day William my brother of 13 years old was taken by the Great Possums on his way from school – and this was all because Daddy was a friend of Mr. Fleischman, a Jewish one who sold to Negroes. I know that William was later found dead by the Chipola River covered in his own blood and his neck slashed like coyotes on a mule and his fishing pole found 30 feet downriver, carried away by the waters, leaving to go anywhere else but Jackson County, I reckon. And me and William used to play jacks with Remus out by the pig pen but we can't no more.

MOSES

There are dead crabs on the beach today
   where the seagulls are bathing.
Death slithers around, pallid,
   the sea-
ports and festoons
   where children throw stones –
       I throw stones
   into the sea
   like a child.

The Red Sea was horrible
but it was beautiful.
It is gone, and I am older now. He
has asked me to be here
and I am.

Serpents come forth from the sea,
   shaking, rattling
my love. I am the confessor.
Where I stand
they circle.
I am unafraid and I am unafraid
 (just as I heard my boy Gershom, his voice, nights ago,
I said *No, this cannot be*)

The sun passes where

no serpent will
   sanctify my love, no
beast will bade me.

I remember there were bodies left
   at pentacost,
the burning bush. There was love
   we have never seen.

And have you seen it, have you seen
there was love here
before there was temptation? that
before temptation there was sin,
before sin we were
babies out here.

I heard Gerhsom's voice nights ago.
   Leave me, son. I haven't heard him since.

and I have been here before, in my dreams, my night-
mares, which I have cast out –
   I have cast *hate* out. I ache. My heart covets that day.

I have set my rod down,
I have laid to rest *hate,*
I have split *hate* into three,
I have chastened fury, when it grew,
I have chastened where my dreams hurt.

I call out my woman's name. Here, I hear it. There it is again, shift-
ing, sinking, slouching, bits torn and carried away – bits lying dead

on top of the bodies on the shore. There is a shift in the way we forgive and be forgiven. I have given heed to that. But my soul will not reach that. I see someone I will never know. I will never know that someone who is coming. I am silent. I feel her, again.

LOCATING THE EDGE

A beatitude
undivined in
statutes and laws.

But that is all that dogs do.
A healer, His palm:
someone is God

for the next two thousand years.
waiting for the time to come,
when on a crackling path

the New Word will hail down
and arrange the world
here on this map.

There is a legend,
there is a territory,
which embraces a border

although it is unsure now,
all the paths washed away
in mud that is unsure and unfounded.

SAMENESS

Every
body
kind
of
does
their own thing, it turns
          out.
Cardinals n squirrels who feed at the same
store, I don't wanna go there, where the workers
sing a song
      about
your birthday. Like everyone they love pointing a camera in your
face. I don't wish to comment on that at this time, though we're
all on the same slop, like we're both saved.

Sameness be my grace, be our grace,
        for once.

&BLOOD

does not care
which way wind
   dirt and worms
   branches and trees go.
& blood does not
attempt dangerous feelings.
& blood cowers in its fury.
& blood is what it is,
        (like a baby with the knife)
so everyone
is beautiful and stupid and unresolved.
               & blood always runs like
little feathers
when flotsam'd and jarred.

Beyond the Wild

No breath in my lungs
nor sleep
inside

these Southern towns,
who harbor
the sun-dried

waves of
the orange cats to me,
like I'm their mother.

I was on the falling
blooms, the drifters
fell

looking at the cats,
saw through the cracking
a fog

of reason,
the shape of nothing
like forms

when these cats get

out their checkbooks,
say, 'Sign here and here,'

like I owed them
something.
Dogwoods askew

and trampled the
cats bucking
I think about

the narcissism
of buds falling their
presentation so smooth,

the big difference
between this and Athens,
between this and that, no

matter if we like it. I love
America b/c it says: love me,
but never as I left you.

What do you want,
my beautiful
ladies?

I hear the seven cats
singing to
the dogwood.

You can't say much about 'virtue.'
It doesn't stir anyone's soul.
          Roses
          don't bleed.

The importance of trash
its ability to forgo the grave.
          Why trash cans are
          gray like the sky

I can't say.

But it couldn't cost much
for you and for me
to keep this in mind:
          for you and for me,
          love is a determined

grasp for shale
afterdeath and thirst
          for melting snow.

One Thing

our hereness a river ancient-
ness an error leagues of red
memories flowing of trees
root vessels inside-
ness an error a river
of memories Being
a great mistake if we had dreamt it
here dreams go / we go unbounded in
that night of objects
human and not
where space is another big thing
among other things

Art bloats life.
Art is cottonfields,
the art of beatings
   & no mercy. & all is indebted
this violence: it is a god against love,
& art redeems all
violence, (oh does it?) but this
is syphilis on our necks –
this is violence we must bear, for now, Satan,
devil of our memory fading

dear God let us out today
to be dead, to not
be dead, to not be
let us out today dear God

Easter present

no sun out
the cow and calf run from it
the rain is coming no trees
no trees to go into trees
let there be a place dear God
they can go tomorrow
the rain is coming tonight
let there be a place dear God

Coup Détat

Jovan Musk
and Angel (hold the star
like a grenade)

Grenada, Senegal, Mambéty and
Sembene: a citrus sting
buzzing bee
pulse

for a birthday cake
rotten body
cake and asshole

a mass shooting rubbed
into my wrists, blade
redrum redrum Gaddafi
helluva Happy Birthday

CHICKENS

1

A child picks at
the wicker chicken
who is standing at attention
plucking feathers stringed
in ropes, draped in locs of
wicker jowls ribboned
around its neck, its beak
clucking just to say exactly nothing
it would not otherwise.

the other chicken is made of metal and is quite sharp and takes his
meals at noontime and will not take it a second

before or after. he enjoys his meal, burps decisively, and rides away
on his motorcycle. he bites children.

yes – the lovely lady
has flown the coop

                    how
regent she is

and I will not tell her

the roosters down there
are missing   are gone

Eau de Parfum

I judge it that your breath is too close to mine and your sweater is touching the space where I could be. Other people's *eau de parfum*. I see you have dropped the small packet of peanuts onto the floor of this airplane. You are not picking it up and your shoes are not laced the same way. I wonder how you could not care in the way that I do that you don't. I figure that the flight I am on will probably experience turbulence, at which point we will jiggle like ballistic dummies who would not survive the crash anyway.

IN TRANSLATION

Honey stays in the hive.

One contortion
of breeze
ran Albion
to New England
under sand
like the feast
at Belshazzar.
Stone face scribbled
in Hebrew

There is 216 again.

Hair caught
in a brush, your pearls
around your neck.

Your hand in a hornet's nest.

And there are the seas.

John Wayne's ass as described by Paul Schrader on the Mishima Director's Commentary track

The rain always mingles with the street garbage – the plastic bags, the spit, the cum, the lube and mucus, the trash of the world washing itself away finally, the leaves red like wine (the color of everything), the garbage and rain washing away beautiful for once, burning in acid rain that's green – the leaves red – in the heat, stuck up like a man's dick in the air, or John Wayne's ass melting into the sunset, the largeness of it the same for men as the women in the desert, the same size as a woman's intuition, who saw through it, in his walking off, his calculations on his heels, to poke out his ass, all of their dreams of his tight ass a cattle's spit, white-hot as steam, blowing out, like a plastic bag over the prairie, as though John Wayne's ass was a weather vane, a crumpling, forlorn vision of how women's kisses dried up in the desert and fucked-off away in the mirror of the land – let's call it dirt – or a cock crowing to the moon, all confused-like, a cock begging for moonlight on the well, where everything beautiful on the frontier was now just retarded.

DRESS-UP

the price of gum
always goes up.
and so does gas
and art.

it costs us something
and we exchange these
these things
between each other. (I think?)
I have the term
it is called currency. (right?)
that is the basic principle
as I understand it.

and there are new ways
to live under it. (or is it in it?)
either way
that is fine with me
that it is always changing

like the way
economists and professors
are always thinking
of new ways to dress-up

the lady. sometimes
they say they'd
like to never have to dress
her at all.

ok
if you say so
I wouldn't care
I'd always end up
thinking about her naked
anyways.

THE GREAT POSSUM

GRANDDADDY SPOKE IN tongues, a language of pentacost. Angel-speak tore through him in convulsions. Often they would begin at dinner – he would shake with motions of fury – but we knew his gift wasn't for us to understand, that neither his body nor ours was anyone's in particular anymore, except as a spectacle to behold.

The table would shake, pounding both fists, Granddaddy speaking a language no one could understand. 'Grab the tablecloth,' Grandma would instruct. I would pinch the tablecloth and pull it from his hands, his fingernails digging into his palm bloody. His spit accumulated like salt and dried in the corner of his mouth like a beach. When he would begin convulsing we would take the fork from his hand so he wouldn't stab it into his eyeballs, as a man a town over had done.

He would float, was the weird thing. His body was a magnet oriented toward God, pushing up, humming. His body heard a frequency; I couldn't hear anything. The hounds yelp. We would nail the chair down to the floor crying. We would tie Granddaddy down to the chair crying. Preacher comes over, to watch: his eyes glass, in incomprehension. 'I cannot make this into something it is not. His gift is beyond me. I wish him the best,' preacher said. There was the idea to charge for Granddaddy's convulsions, as a spectacle to behold. But enough money is made off blood, I thought. I would ask Granddaddy why he spoke in tongues.

What did he have to gain from it, his strange connection. What did God say to him? 'It was not God, but the Great Possum.' He wouldn't answer anymore, making a remark about the sun setting over the oak trees – the pecans would begin falling soon, and would roll around then stop, never to move again.

I only tell Granddaddy I hope it is not a gift from the devil.

And he would never answer.

OPENING THE JAR

My ass on the sand, I have fingernails now / for what it's worth. / and some people put sand in a jar / and some people put toenails in a jar. / My toes crawling on the shore / the shore crawling on my footprints. / It goes down, I don't know why, it fills my footprints. / I get sand under my fingernails now / and dead skin that I pick out with floss / but the truth is, most of the time, I use my teeth / so I get sand in my teeth and / I only have fingernails on my right hand. / And often I think that Jesus really left the footprints.

everyone rebels in the cage
but let us not get too po-

– litical. *liturgical?*
   the word
should be dear to us
'look away, look away, look away, look away,'
it goes.

side – charcoal – brick: three words which you need from
         here-on-out. don't
give a rats' about it, that fair to assume? not
that an essay on the subject will suffice
but it is a start.
it was written down, told, has age.
I was taught thus: to meet-cute, with an axe, you yielded a hefty
wife and sev'ral acres of land! a mule to keep happy! or so.
or so is the word.

or so. Swingers of,
other axe-grinders, homesteaders
in the ancient evening, lived through-
out the ancientness, were fore-
told a fundamental

sex. everything is worse
back in tha cage, and it spins like the world!

yes, of course it does, as though
(I repeat myself)

it would ever do anything else.
in that case we

are one to be born again,
in the river of fundament, my boy.
that is, my boy, all things, all points of history
coming to a head.

JOHN WILKES BOOTH

As tempting as the thought of interrupting this actor talking about
Venice Preserv'd was, I placated myself in the corner against a shelf, a
stack of books, his name not known to me then, him leaning against
that shelf of books about economics, monetary theory, history.

Then there arrived some words to me, which were that he could con-
vince me God existed in some way other than what I knew, and I in-
terrupted, but he said, 'Oh, I won't, no, that's not – '

' – that is not really for me to force upon you, no, no, I don't
think, but I, I will leave you alone, now, near the other young
sheep. you know the name they have for them, you know?'

Newborns. Right. Whatever could that mean.

He says, *No, that's not – anyhow –*

> imagine a house with no roof and, look-at-there,
> it is not one house, not one –
> not one worth living, anyhow
> *in* anyway, so there would not be,
> to my eyes, any particular reason for
> you to stoke the chimney, it's
>
> like you're Lincoln now!
> oh, just wonderful.

but even Lincoln would not leave
if his assassin arrived.

Oh, John Wilkes Booth, I know of you. We know you. You interrupt our processions and parading of micemen, who belabor their spirit toward their compass, the ground, this small town the earth their ears tasting, speaking in foreign tongues (voices say 'Force us to stop'), but their voices falling, dozing, somnambulant and gray, clop on the cement of a new town like bricks falling, its bricks engraved with Latinate nudes of women, once, down the main street now replaced by murals of local plants, where stopping at the drug store you, Booth, had ordered I think it was two chocolate milkshakes, and you sipped them, walking back down to the building which was no store (housed, in fact, all of the widow's art supplies – that was Booth there, stopping again, as he dusts off his shoulders to tell me that I don't know anything at all about history. 'But I've somewhere to be tonight,' says Booth, mysteriously.

He reminds me – he reminds me I will know the dictates of history on his terms soon enough. I told Booth, I told him, I don't need no coming-to. I know what I know.

oh, where are the deer
deer had the trees cut
down a couple years before deer died
what deer did with the money was they
hid it in the fuel tank of their tractor
where are the deer now? they've
retreated into the woods
like jellyfish.
time was flat, and deer couldn't
go forward or backward, like on string,
deer were always pressed against glass,
so close the clouds began to squat
and hit deer heads with its knees,
like a father who drank the light bill
away, and this was why deer had to wash their clothes
in the river and scrub them against stones –
the kinds of stones deer'd hide on top of gas pumps
to see if they'd still be there when deer came back,
where deer'd hide between the aisles and take
Bar-S hotdogs stole from an 8-pack,
gas smell deer came to know as river fish
laying eggs as they surged beneath the brook,
same sense of time as squeezing under,
like primordial life when they used to fight.

KILLING GOMER PYLE

Gomer Pyle is a darkling,
lured beneath America's soul.

He finds the underbelly everywhere.
He cannot imagine a world so cruel that would have him.

He is good and he can die real good.
He talks funny and he can die real good.

He is retarded and he can die real good.
He is a hick and he can die real good.

Sitting in the pit of your stomach, stay there,
and wrap yourself around his musings.

From yonder there Gomer Pyle waves,
oblivious because of course he is.

Lenin, Stalin, and Hitler

If it was not clear that I only think about men: I only think about men. Men make my ceiling fan spin. Men listen to my conversation in the other room. Men make my walls thin. Somehow, men can see between my blankets. Men own mortars and pestles. When I read a book about Lenin, Stalin, and Hitler, I learn about Lenin, Stalin, and Hitler. If only there was everything to know about them, maybe medicine balls wouldn't deflate and seeds would find their way out of my fruit.

Fast Car

Take you in my fast car we   take time we

can go anywhere in the city   it's a dump

take you out to feel on your dick   fast car

I drive in and out I leave   can't take us to

isolation is queerness I reject   queerness

Guy I go to the dump to says   goodbye like

he fell in a woman's   makeup bag

I reject isolation I just   drive the car

HYSTERIAS

hysterias
in me. *oh*. so
this is the dishwasher
my dad's hysterias
is I am never the people
who tell me what I
         want to hear.
my mom's hysterias
are not simpler / they are
easier to understand because she is
my mother. but they are not easier to
triangulate. this is the dilemma.
it's so that every thought of me
ends in chanting against Oedipus.

         in other words, 'mys' weigh nothing
and life isn't measured in years
but in hysterias.

it's so boring.

being here is actually boring
         and boring is always worse than the other.
         and what's scary is

how
it isn't.

the main thing I do is keep my cards
close between memory and me

KING KONG

no crying dear no crying   in the chair
where you sit w/ me and taste   my fingers
trace them and suck me I   taste your tears
falling down your flannel   suck them off
I make myself   leave you

I wander   down your street
and take you   for granted
I visit   little shops
and buy you   blue china
in Tallahassee
I walk in mud
         making you tea
         I watch you drink it

you wear   pretty crazy outfits
my favorite is when   you were frozen in ice
you cleaned the dishes by hand   let me taste your fingers
your never wear your rings   that's what I like about you
but your chair feels   it's been wrestled in
it has known I was here   place our rings
in the bowl   your hands in mine

above your *King Kong* poster   doesn't that tell you
everything you need to know?

I GUESS I REMEMBER THINGS MORE CLEARLY WHEN I'M WITH YOU

Show me what I really want to see.
That's cereal with water, I
can't drink milk without running
to the bathroom. Talking
is not about speech, it's
about how your shoulders dip
when I touch you or kiss
your neck on its nape now.
I pick you up the same
time I always did at the store,
I take your clothes off in the
shower and flush them down
our toilet while you pin your
hair up in that way you always
did that makes me think of the
Super Bowl. I could never
understand how you
kept your dry
in the shower.
But I guess I remember things
more clearly
now that there are things
about you I could not know.

CATTLE

I'm cattle for you

The Past Comes Back To Haunt Us All

The past comes back to haunt us all.
Ghost of ghosts' past in haunting
blue-ish cum bodies,
   life-suckers.
Ghosts are what were not
inquisitors, once – who I know I knew.
They ask you about your body
and the relation to it like we
have a body: it's nothing to *have* a body,
and hasn't since last year. You must have
someone else confused with my body;
I done changed the description. I'm not
gay anymore, and music sounds different
to me in the dark when I don't know
what the genitals are; I don't even care.
About my nothing there is none,
   no change.
Because what is that.
I exist or I don't, or and I don't,
and I've never met
anyone who knew the things as I was:
some ghost hacked me, sent their
feelings I was so unclear about.

Where was I a ghost now that those things came out?
   Where weren't I would be the better question.
   I think 'ghosts' and 'hauntings' are retarded.

You are visited by God and you appreciate it,
you are not scared of it totally.
It is one to 'ghost,'
        another to *be* 'ghost.'
I see them all the time walking the street.
I don't admire them for their blue-ish cum body,
As such.
Likewise I don't miss my grandfather at all:
I see him twice a week
        at stores where
        people disappear into other aisles
        and are never seen again.

Talking about talking to the dead, you wouldn't clear it as *God* but
me if I wasn't: a thought, feelings that went way beyond normal,
against some membrane to push against. In the end we found out
the nothing I was after meant fuck-all, but it was the only word that
described everything. *This right here.* Why would we ever change any-
thing when it got here exactly as it was. Or is. So all of their ques-
tions and gestures don't mean anything to me.

INALIENABLE

mom
not that I should use the term I would rather not use,
you, or *she*, I guess, but mom fell out of her wheelchair
and it was not surprising, no –
no expressions of shock or that I threw my things
into the sea, (gaping face of) in Rome –
no wish, as it were.
How cruel is it to be necessary?
I don't understand how
time and suffering haven't fished.
Slide your fingers inside a fish or a man,
or a woman, say, 'well God I don't get it,' not to say
I could, but I'd die every single day (I think someone took my
pills today and that is one thing for certain, like Death)
The beauty of it all is that I'd get jealous
because I'd suddenly know what's for real.

RICHARD NIXON

As a matter of course, oh
looks don't count that much, so I,
I don't know, don't mind if I haven't seen myself in a while, I find
myself, again, on this *island*, as always, and
   Oh, God, I am in
   awe! My skull,
      my face, my meat, my clams, my feet,
      my shoes wait for you to goddamn tie them, to thatch my
      hut, to carve me some sort of idol. You sick people,
      who lit my torch and
      burnt the forest, the sea snakes, coconuts.

(What I learned, early, was that eels –
      God bless them – were
      meant just to swim. Do not eat them.)
If you were not first, as first is, you grew
immune from the appeal of townhouses, brick-
      laid amenities, like my grandfather carried himself
(a house tall, and strong,
                 and ancient, and efficient, and
indifferent to
      time, and today's morality, and pain-
      fullness. the fascists flung themselves through time.
        the rivers, the forests, the seas, the natives

were abstracted, like crab shells, railroads, Chinamen,

wicker chairs, Corinthian columns, master
bedrooms, the lips of a cunt – or cock hole, fishnets, pennies in
fountains – and seagulls, lapping the urinals at Shea Stadium.

About the slave-quarters,
        witchcraft, voodoo, burning idols:
if you ask me honestly these are all foreign to me, and for that I
        am said to be against party line, not quite ethical.

Well what could you possibly know
if you knew what I knew?

GHOST (SO WHAT)

       so what
if I'm person or
or someone I'm ghost

       where were
you when I was
on the roof of my house

       staring
blank at pink
oval pink clouds I'm ghost

       I am
ghost before
ideas threw me beads

       flowers
I spent college time
gardening roses

       about
what it means
to be good to people

more than
in economics
I'm capitalist

that means
I ask God for
money and He says no

here is
another for you
God it's a little tougher

will I
have child with wife
or is that just for thee

my wife
locked up Miami
General Hospital

it's not
at all what you'd think
a perfect cup of coffee

from the
hospital vending
machine is twenty cents

there are
better uses of
hands than for building

prisons
of my own design
I just know I'll die

when they
hand him to me bloody
screaming and kicking mad

and she
crying while I think
think about Michael Jordan

section
C is for clean-open
Now a week in

after
couldn't taste Jell-O
couldn't taste nothing

except
what she tastes when
she wakes up

she ate
baby she ate good real
real good just like you

babies
not supposed to eat
pickles but I let her anyhow

am I
even doing this
right this how you hold the

bottle
this how you do it
I think she takin it right

God He
exists this I know but
I'm prepared for Him

to not
care that I know
don't press me for it

Bulls won
against the Knicks
in six I remember

Have to
to settle in soon
to this I'm ghost I know

nothing
about nothing
then again so what?

MY SON

Stupid
thought that I could be
someone's father

but I
do have it. It's just
I'm 'unfit for service.'

how gay
guys come about we
come about like sharks

slowly
and then it's too late
I'd tell my son about sharks

he'd say
'You can't really me
that you for real saw a shark

really
show me a shark then
on this map of Florida

looks like

a shark if he bent
himself over and scratched

his gills.'
I'd tell him I'd touched the gills
before and they didn't feel right.

'Tonight
a shark exits the sea
a prude he's done with

all the
naked people coming
into his house'

my son
would laugh at that joke
if I ever had one

he'd have
my sense of humor
and laugh at that joke

and find
things like sharks stupid
though they are not.

TITANIC

The sound of the planets circling
lilies

The sound of a new problem
not fixed by *you*
    do you know how quick
    it goes bad
    if you don't
    plug the hole?

They cannot see us
floating turbu
   -Lent

it's all written down on
palms
psalms

  (scribbled
napkin thoughts
on Ash Wednesday)

    all's forgiven
    all's forgotten
    of Eve, who sank

        the Titanic,
launching an ancient ship
out to sea, winking.

    (God says *tut-tut*,
really, to that.

His number, which I have saved in my phone, is
        c-o-n-f-i-d-a-n-t;
        to wit
        a pseudo
        -nym
that is easier to swallow.

Bunny Rabbit

Finger split down to my bone
My bone juts irresponsibly
Wrong colors my bones out
Try telling a nurse all about it
She tell me, 'Why can't the sky
Be another color as your bones?' I say
My bone showing (a muscle chasm,
Blood split in my body, between
Dark and congealed dying earth)
'No, that's not why, not why at all –
Who let Bunny out?
Why Bunny out?'
Bunny think pouring acid down your brain
Make you his sex slave. 'Oh.'
But Bunny been out couple years.
'Well what's the difference between bone and its skin'
She sew me up, she say
(Hills and muscle *plink*-ing guitar strings)
'So he the reason we don't have Easter no more.'
Pretty much.
I kneel out on the porch
Dripping blood, proud of it.

Sickness

I KNEW NO ONE at the exhibition had come to see my paintings. They had come to see the paintings of Mike Apel, 30 and rich, some of it his daddy's, sophisticated enough to not find himself struggling near the bottom rung. He huffed the faintest fumes of legacy.

The Apels were from South Africa and his father became enamored with Gertrude Stein when the family relocated to New York. You couldn't see the influence in Mike's work; what I saw was freedom.

He wanted to belong to performance painting. The act of painting itself, performing it, was his notion of radicality that I on the whole wasn't opposed to. He thrilled Yoko Ono, who attended one of his shows. He had rid himself of bourgeois, painterly aesthetics. He was free of those delusions that haunted the art world.

Primrose Stefanski curated the show. A portly woman with thin, red glasses. She wears cowprint jackets, blouses, pants, shoes, bags. Her face was thin, her body was fat, and she repulsed me. I found power in admitting that.

Mike approached me three weeks ago because he knew I would kill, because he knew I was capable of it. Splitting my time between writing and painting was excruciating and I had this pain that had wrapped itself around my brain. There was agreement on that between us. But why come to violence, I asked.

There was no answer. The silence ensnared me – I was mothlike – but I soon had felt the pain arrive to my temples. The thought of seeing him dead on the floor was too much. I afforded myself the comfort of knowing it hadn't happened yet.

So for the following three weeks I maintained my composure,

knowing the show was going to happen. Was there any pain? Only infrequently, but I staved off any thoughts about what was expected of me. My great task. The whole point of the art world was no longer to find new artists but to kill them all. That must have been his point.

Our conversation had melted away into nothing. I remembered few details and I questioned if it had even happened. I had sent this to Prim that week and she had approved it quick, but it was all true:

[My name]'s work as a white artist interrogates the roots of ethnography as personal inquiry, self-actualization, and "decolonization." Their paintings often include subjects about Western notions of rootedness, discovery, and post-colonial exploitation that intersect with improvisation as politics.

I stood near the de Koonings and felt small; I shrank. I slipped out the door; entombed, I vomit in the street and lay in it for a while. I don't remember.

My lyrics to a chorus I misheard

Dunce
Dunce
Dunce
Dunce
Dunce
Dunce
Dunce
Dunce
Dunce
Dunce
Dunce
Dunce
With me

The Bridesmaids

They are Southern – their facts justify everything.

Their black faces are delicately painted,
renderings of grace, smoothed-out and hollow;
   they hate the reception – they'd rather
   search the yard for chicken eggs, tow their
   grandbabies in a potato sack, field another drop of
sweat from the plow.

The artist, naturally, is a white woman gives them an unnatural
glow; big shapes, impressive; large women, with stature. In the
room huge beings can't help but hear

      every creak in the floor, as you gathered your wits
      about them – these bridesmaids' are stoic,
      upturned, possibly sour at the thought of me staring

at them so rudely – maybe it was the thought of being at someone
else's wedding in the sweltering Alabama heat that did them
in, left them so inhospitable to peace from another white face,
another white stare.

Was it me or the Muse who knew me better than to present
   some notion in a place so hostile to the unyielding
   stampede of history?

OVERTHREW

Sunday is humid.
I have to work 7 days
to get off 3. I'll
be with you
then. I'm sorry,
it's Monday really,
but I'll be there.
I'm a tick on a dog. I've come
to reject the feeling
of my loneliness, mine,
as a strange decadence
for you.
I really don't like this feeling.
Read a poem about
a broken coffee pot.
Didn't like it. So
humid today I'm pretty
sure humidity is a
necessary factor in
worldwide oppression.
I'm pretty sure.
I don't really care. I see everything
in old books and anapests now,
the sharpness of broken glass.
Kiss me pregnant. Then pause.
You said kissing me

is barely kissing me
because you don't know
where I stand on politics.
I couldn't think of something
worse to say to someone.
These oak trees have not
once complained to me
like you do.
I forget, now,
where once a thing
happened here, in this place –
all this sweat for nothing, no
distance between
your intentions to mine.

PIG IS COW

I give back the writing as some mistake. Glazed donut world intrigued by all the holes of which, some sort of sickness man to man to hole that writing down feeds a wet nurse. now sexy.

I can't enjoy pigs anymore because I eat them sexy, so I hate pigs and hope they die for me, and they do. I'm vegan now, sexy. Won't touch the pork anymore. Am pretty sure the pig is holy and so is cow.

I give back the writing, this. I have created its unwritten other self which ends, a smooth white shape of nothing that is everything. Pig is cow.

THE SOURCE OF LIFE

our new antenna pointed eastward
toward the Florida aquifer which ran underneath
a bowling alley in a documentary in the 5th grade

there was no question at least from me about the body then
and the body still isn't particularly interesting except for its
    entrances
still rots and falls apart

make a reminder for me to keep my will
pointed toward someone more alive than me
more hair on their head less fat on their frame

a beautiful youth who really don't even know
what Coca-Cola is or why someone
would have any interest in it

beyond how much
it would take to
kill someone like me

There will be a time when you are all alone and there will be nothing you can do about it

SHED BEHIND THE WOODS a chicken house, the beams slatted on top, painted pink. These have protective properties, this pink, of rain and weather. High grass, I add, protects the snakes too. I know. And then he ask why ain't the grass done away with and I don't give any answer. These things get away with me. 'We can save these shells for the chickens to eat.' 'Sea shells?' (NO, RETARD). We haven't any chickens yet. 'We haven't answer snakes yet either' – I lie. We do have them, but we (including 'I') know not where they are. Sense they are always there. Know not where from they arrive. Pond, as it is, must be filled with new fish, and we ask not for any snakes during the summer. They cross the road. Unwanted certainly. Washing machine grass terraforms, abandoned. We in the dump.

The land makes way for us, you know. The climate adjusts, not changes. How many tools do you have in there, Father? I would not mind counting for you. If I knew there weren't snakes.

So the chicken house will be pink. Is that amendable? – no jokes about 'fags' or whatever. Strong moral compass. Good. You shall be pliable for some new order, where I can't be myself. Moccasins swim with their heads only poking out the water little. Blow them away with shotgun. Deadly at short range: everything is exactly the same in that way already. Need to eradicate difference not necessary, ordained already. Need for it safety like a big oak tree falls. One is the back of the house, one is front. Thoughts of it falling down on me. It is me mostly after all who does the dying in my dreams. But no one will listen to me about memories of men with nightmares of doing terrible and hateful things to women and children in the jungle and in the desert. Know not if they were real or not. I will reassure myself. Must get rid of. But won't. Truth is: everything is real – a terrible thought.

Money was reason thereof for disappearance of trees out back. We sold to him, he said he'll make some trees grow again. Eventually. How many times I must explain that. Big field all of a sudden disappears, it's not the worst thing to history, to have had happened.

There was the impression that is it was important for men and women to disappear once. Then *again*, greedily. Came back home and they were *different*, with new memories of the things they had made people do. Same 'person' returned is difficult to say. What even is it to be the same person or different person. Change is always a smoothed out, like ice cream. I believe to believe in that when minds came together in which the differences between men and women returned is when change happened.

Know a guy who says he sat on Saddam Hussein's golden toilet. Not sure I believe in toilets like that. What else does he know that he was prepared for? It's not so much change as something unlocked maybe. So *returned* is inaccurate. *Abducted*, more like. Likewise this is not much my voice, but my voice similarly inhabits I; what inhabits I *is*.

School I went to got sold to a lumber mill – not *my* school, I should say, because I would not ever want responsibility of telling anyone something they didn't already want to know to do; no one needs to know what to do. Long time ago, would have had freakout over such. Something unlocked maybe. All I know for sure is that where I go we go. I began to think responsibility is too much for anyone to have. As an old saying goes you never do anything on your own. There will be a time when you're all alone and there will be nothing you can do about it. Even the slightest hand will graze a cheek and feel that.

About the Author

HAYDEN CHURCH is editor of *Maximus Magazine*. His poetry, flash fiction, and essays have been published in *Apocalypse Confidential*, *Don't Submit!*, *Misery Tourism*, *Safety Propaganda*, *Bear Creek Gazette*, *Azure Bell*, *PopMatters*, and *Splice Today*. He lives in Florida.

YOU, THE VIEWER AT HOME, MOON
TOM WILL

COLLECTED POEMS (*coming soon*)
WALLACE BARKER

DECAY NEVER BEGAN (*coming soon*)
DAVID KUHNLEIN